WATER AND TEA

Water and Tea

Disconnect to Reconnect

KEAGAN AUSTIN

Finally Aligned

This book is based on the experiences of the writer with the sole purpose of bringing awareness to the true power of fasting. The writer intends to share his experience in hopes that you too will choose a similar path when faced with the difficulties of life.

This book is available on Amazon, Barnes and Nobles, and all other media platforms, but it will always be FREE at www.WaterAndTeaBook.com

Contents

Chapter 1

Introduction

"So you want me to starve myself on purpose?" This is the question I would ask when presented with the idea of fasting. I could not wrap my head around the idea of purposely going without food. "You do it to get closer to God," people would often respond, only regurgitating what had been regurgitated to them. "No, I'm good," I would reply. "I pray and read my bible. God is not trippin' about my McChicken's," and I would continue on with my day. However, as I matured and got older, something inside of me longed for a deeper and more intimate connection with God. I found myself wanting to be more than a bible skimmer and 'God is Good, God is Great' grace prayer.

As a child, I was deeply rooted in the Baptist church. I played the keyboard, was a youth usher, and even sang in the kids' choir. As a teenager, I began to stray away from the gospel music I was accustomed to and started making music of my own outside of church, primarily Hip Hop/Rap. Due to the values instilled in me while growing up in church, I could always feel God pulling at my heart every time I would drift too far with my music content. When this occurred, I would always reconstruct the song and lyrics to better fit who I was as a person and not the people I was trying to impress. As a rapper, I was no Lecrae but I wasn't Too Short either, I was more like a 'Too-crae'. I stayed true to myself letting my thoughts flow freely, creating music I was proud of.

After college, I spent years performing and inspiring people to be themselves. The main message I tried to convey was that "L.A.M.E" (Living According to My Expectations) was actually the new "Cool". People of all ages and nationalities would gravitate to the messages in my music and I knew it was God that allowed me to have that level of impact and influence on everyone I met. I spent years traveling and performing, but not too long after having my daughters, Kadence and Joelle, I started to question if I was using my time on earth wisely. Time, as we all know, is the one thing you can never get back. It can't be manipulated with money, and it doesn't care about your success. When your time is up, your time is up. So, I started asking myself, am I truly being productive with the gifts God has given me? I always felt music was my gift. Doors opened when music was involved, but my new question was "Am I fulfilling my purpose?". Was I truly fulfilling the task God created me for or was

I out of alignment simply doing something I had become good at?

At this point of my life, my prayer life was very inconsistent, and I had pretty much stopped going to church all together. I was probably averaging 5 Sundays a year (6 if my mom happened to be in town) and was really in need of real direction and guidance. So, I said what every back-sliding Christian says when they feel they need to get back on track, "I gotta start going back to church!". I made up my mind that church would be my new Sunday routine like it used to be when I was younger, then BOOM.... Covid-19 hit, and EVERYONE had to stop going to church. So, there I was, locked down in quarantine with no sense of purpose, no true direction, just a burning desire to connect with God.

During lock down, I stopped making music all together because I wondered if it was distracting me from my actual purpose. Every day I would watch sermons on YouTube by Michael Todd, Dr. Myles Munroe, and Tim Ross. I was very particular on what I allowed to enter my mind, because I was taught that every preacher of God is not a preacher from God. Diving into Gods word consistently opened up my mind like never before. I began to have a better understanding of God outside of religious routines. I began to have a better understanding of love, grace and forgiveness, learning how to properly pray, and even the true reason on why we pay tithes. Each day that passed, I was becoming more and more enlightened about The Most High and the bible.

After 6 straight months of consistently being in the word of God, my faith became stronger than it had ever been, but I was still no closer to understanding my individual purpose in life. Around this time, there was one sermon that caught my attention while scrolling through YouTube. It was titled, "Prayer and Fasting Consecration" by Dr. Myles Monroe. I had come a long way from being the kid who would pass up on God's presence for a Mc-Chicken, and I found myself planning my first true fast in hopes to get clarity on a few things in my life.

Chapter 2

The Fast

I once attempted what I thought was a "fast" but after listening to that sermon, I realized I had done it completely wrong. Back when I first tried it, I fasted and continued with my daily routines like going out, watching television, performing, social media, etc. During those times, whenever hunger struck, I would turn to distractions instead of prayer and reading the word of God. I even found myself focusing more on weight loss, than positioning myself to hear God's voice. There was no real transformation, it was more of a quick diet solution. I later found out, while reading Isaiah 58:3-4, that continuing with daily routines/distractions are the exact fast God ignores.

Isaiah 58:3-4,
"Why have we fasted,' they say,
'and you have not seen it?
Why have we humbled ourselves,
and you have not noticed?'
"Yet on the day of your fasting, you do as you please
and exploit all your workers.
4 Your fasting ends in quarreling and strife,
and in striking each other with wicked fists.
You cannot fast as you do today
and expect your voice to be heard on high."

This time around, my fast would be done correctly and intentionally, by diligently seeking Gods presence and removing all distractions.

Fasting is a way to refocus the spirit by removing all distractions and mental roadblocks. In the bible, Samuel, Ezra, Esther, Elijah, Daniel, Paul, John the Baptist, and Jesus all fasted. When you fast, you are not only resetting your body, but also telling the flesh that it is no longer in control. It is not all about food, it is about removing the influences our daily activities have on our thoughts and mind, allowing God's voice to cut through all of the unnecessary background noise. We need to isolate ourselves from people, things, and situations that play to our desires, or our flesh, that disconnect us from our natural state, which is spirit.

On a biological level, while fasting from food, your body is eagerly looking for sugars to convert into energy, and when it cannot find any, your body begins to eat away at itself converting fat to energy. This is why you lose weight while fasting. You are literally taking your flesh to its weakest state to connect with the spirit which is your highest form. You are silencing your own self-serving voice to hear God's voice. Fasting shows God we are willing to ignore natural instincts to eat, just to hear his voice and be in his presence for a moment.

After finishing the sermon "Prayer and Fasting Consecration" by Dr. Myles Monroe, I was all in and began reading up on all the different types of fast, in the bible, to figure out which fast would be best for me. My first thought was to do the Daniel fast (Daniel 1:8-14), which only removes meat from your diet. But looking back to 2017, when I went vegan with the rest of the world after watching "What the Health", I realized that I could probably do that in my sleep. The fast would last 2 months, but only removing meat would not be a real sacrifice for me. Paul went 3 days with no food or water (Acts 9:9), but with me being a beginner faster, I heard a voice deep down in my spirit say, "You ain't bout that life!" (Translation: You're not ready for that). So, I decided to do a 7 day fast with water and tea only. No fruit, no vegetables, no meat, just water and tea for 7 days. Here were the details of my fast:

Consumption:
Water and Tea Only
Restrictions:
Television
Social Gatherings
Checking Stocks/Crypto
Checking All Social Media
YouTube Videos (not related to the fast)

Now that the framework of my fast was set; it was now time to focus on the most important part of the fast, which was detailing my 'it'. Your 'it' is whatever you are seeking God for. What do you need revealed? What is it you need better clarity on? It is a very intimate prayer, right before your fast (and throughout) stating exactly why you are seeking his presence. Without intentionality, you aren't truly fasting (in a biblical sense) you're just on an extreme diet. My prayer went like this:

"God, I ask that You give me strength as I enter something I have never entered before. I ask that You speak to me in ways we have never spoken before and guide me in the direction that follows Your will and not my own. I pray for understanding of my purpose, not my own desires, but the purpose You created me for. God, I ask that whatever is revealed, that You make it clear and direct so that I do not miss it. I ask that You give me clarity on the relationships in my life that need to be revived and those that need to be buried. Help me to see the difference between a distraction and the wife You have handpicked for me to help fulfill Your purpose. Amen."

The following entries contain the clarification I received during my fast. Some of the things revealed coincide directly with my 'it' prayer, while others were unexpected but gave a better understanding of the word of God and increased my faith. This was supposed to be a private journal to reference back to once my fast was over, but on Day 5 it was evident God had another plan.

Chapter 3

The Garden

Going into the fast, I was not only struggling with identifying my purpose, but I was at the end of yet another failed relationship and I could not figure out what was wrong. Why were all my relationships ending in a similar fashion? Why would they start so promising only to end with me feeling like my partner wasn't capable of being what I needed? Were they truly incapable or was I coming to the table incomplete, looking for someone to fill a void only God could fill? After meditating and really reflecting on the details of my past, I realized that the last time I was truly single would probably date all the way back to my 10th grade year of high school. If I wasn't in a official relationship, then there was always a 'friend', a 'situation-ship', or 'friend with benefits' that was not too far away. Whenever one relationship ended, things would just seem to fade right into the next. After doing the math, I realized that this was literally the first time in 17 years that I was truly by myself single-single. During my fast, I did a lot of self-analyzation and broke down both my strengths and weaknesses. Understanding how my strengths and weaknesses have helped and hindered my relationships in the past. While praying my "it" prayer, I asked God to help me to identify distractions in regard to the women in my life. I honestly expected Him to just tell me, "Tammy is the one and Keisha is a bum", but He had a completely different approach in how He wanted to get the message across. He did this by taking me all the way back to the first relationship ever recorded, Adam and Eve.

When we were taught the story of Adam and Eve, the main part that is usually pointed out is that God created Eve for Adam. Then the serpent tricked Eve and she ate the fruit, triggering the fall of man. When you take a deeper look into scripture, a lot happened before Eve even comes into the picture. Let me show you:

Genesis 2:7[7] Then the Lord God formed a man[a] from the dust of the ground and breathed into his nostrils the breath of life, and the man became a living being.

If I were God, I would have noticed right then and there that Adam was alone and needed some company, but God said not yet.

Genesis 2:15-17[15] The Lord God took the man and put him in the Garden of Eden to work it and take care of it. [16] And the Lord God commanded the man, "You are free to eat from any tree in the garden; [17] but you must not eat from the tree of the knowledge of good and evil..."

Now there are 2 things God made Adam aware of in these verses. Adam had a clear understanding of why he was created and what his purpose was before Eve was even a thought. God created Adam, put him in the garden, and told him to work it and take care of it. Secondly, God gave him "rules" to abide by. *"You are free to eat from any tree in the garden; but you must not eat from the tree of the knowledge of good and evil".* Adam, the individual, was already walking in his purpose and following God's rules, or commandments before a woman was ever brought to the table. Only THEN did God say in verse 18,

"It is not good for the man to be alone. I will make a helper suitable for him."

There are prerequisites in your single life that need to be met before you should even think about being in a relationship with someone else. Adam was in God's presence, following God's rules and was given a clear understanding of his purpose. He was spending real 1 on 1 time with the creator and then God presented him with a helper which he made his wife. So here's the tough question I had to ask myself. Seeing that this fast is the first time I've spent real time in God's presence, was I ever previously qualified to have girlfriends?

"I will make a helper suitable for him."

If a man is unaware of his purpose, what can a woman help him with? A man with no direction can only lead a woman nowhere. Being able to provide does not necessarily mean a man understands his purpose. It just means he knows how to make money. This is why some of the wealthiest people are unhappy and live unfulfilled lives. Purpose is revealed when it is just you and God alone in the garden. That 1 on 1 time in the garden becomes the foundation of your relationships to come. I spent 17 years, in and out of relationships, trying to find fulfillment in vibes, energy, and sometimes even sex, when all I needed to do was take a seat in the garden and wait for further instructions. Could it be possible that the reason most of our relationships fail is because we've left the garden before we were instructed. Or maybe you keep investing into partners who have not spent enough time in the garden and those bad eggs keep ruining good omelets. Purpose was intended to be revealed to us in our single state with no distractions, but most of us leave the garden prematurely and choose to just "thug it out" in unsanctioned relationships that lead to nowhere.

This concept of maximizing your singleness was not new to me. I had heard it preached twice before, by both Dr. Myles Munroe and Michael Todd, and never applied it to my own life. It was not until the third time, during the fast, that it really resonated with me and became clear. God wants me to be so focused on my purpose that relationships are not even a thought. Adam never asked for Eve, he was too busy doing what needed to be done in the garden. God presented Eve only after Adam met the requirements of the single life and not before. Culture will tell you to date around until you find the one, but they never speak on the prerequisites needed before entering the dating scene. The prerequisites you need to meet in your single season are being in God's Presence, being under God's Provision, and working to fulfill God's Purpose in your life. Women who are unaware of these prerequisites usually settle for men who have never been in the garden and make it their life's project to help him discover himself. It is not a woman's job to help a man discover his purpose, she should be adding on to the vision that has already been revealed. The second part of all of this is that God did not present Eve until she was complete and fully equipped to be a suitable helper for Adam. Adam did not complete Eve and Eve did not complete Adam; they were completed by God while they were individuals, then brought together to assist each other in fulfilling purpose.

Chapter 4

The Heart is not "Heart"

The heart is often associated with deep feelings, emotions, and love. The Old Testament, in particular, refers to the heart often.

Samuel 16:7
*"The lord looks at the **heart**".*
Proverbs 4:23
*"Above all guard your **heart** for everything flows from it"*
Deuteronomy 6:5
*"Love God with all your **heart**".*

We assume, based on our understanding and modern definition, that when 'heart' is mentioned in the bible, it is referring to emotions or feelings. When reading from the original Hebrew text, we find out that this is not the case at all.

The original text, of the Old Testament, was written in Hebrew. Over time, the text has been translated into a multitude of different translations (It is important to note that I am only referencing the Old Testament because some of the New Testament was written in Greek and does not apply). The Hebrew word for 'heart' actually means 'the mind' or 'subconscious thoughts'. So, when reading passages from the Old Testament, the 'heart' is not referring to your emotions or feelings, it is speaking in regard to your state of mind and your thoughts. This information changes everything! The understanding of this is very important because the misunderstanding leads to misinterpreting God's word and intent. When you read a scripture like Proverbs 4:23, *"Above all guard your **heart** for everything flows from it"*, it is not telling you to guard your emotions/feelings, but instead it is telling you to beware of what you subject your mind to and what you feed your thoughts (conversations, music, images etc.). So, with proper understanding of 'heart', that same scripture would be read like this, "Above all protect your mind because everything flows from it".

Satan is the king of distorting the truth. Satan knows that if he can distort your understanding, you will forever travel down the wrong path, in confidence, based on distorted truth. If the devil can get you to believe that God speaks to you through your feelings and emotions, then you will begin to be led by your feelings and emotions. You will begin to listen more to your flesh over your thoughts/conscience.

Our mind and our emotions are always in constant conflict with each other. You hear people say all the time, "My heart is telling me one thing, but my mind is telling me something different". And because of Satan's ability to distort truth, the accepted response to this statement is usually, "Go with your heart" which is actually suggesting that you go with your fleshly instinct. How many times have you honestly heard that? We ignore the internal voice connected to our spirit, to take advice from people who are just as misguided as we are. In most cases solely following your heart will leave you broken in the end saying, "I should have gone with my first thought". Paul writes, *"Who has known the mind of the lord that he may instruct Him? But we have the mind of Christ" (1 Corinthians 2:16).* When we align with God, his thoughts and plans start manifesting through us. We must refocus our minds every day to fully understand what He is trying to communicate.

Chapter 5

The Seen vs. The Unseen

The bible says that we are made in Gods image. If God is a spirit, making us in His image would mean He hand crafted our spirits to be identical to His. People tend to value their bodies over their spirit because our bodies are visible, and our spirit is not. We dress up our bodies in the most expensive clothes, spend thousands of dollars on surgeries and alterations, even base a person's value on their outer appearance, but it is our spirit that should be treated with the highest level of importance. Our physical bodies are the suits our spirit functions in while here on earth, while our spirit is our direct link to the creator. The understanding of The Seen vs. The Unseen, or commonly referred to as The Flesh vs. The Spirit, was a revelation I did not expect to receive during my fast, but it was much needed and right on time.

Similar to our mind and our emotions, the 'spirit' and the 'flesh' are also in a constant battle. Our flesh is led by what it can see, feel (emotions), hear, and touch. Whereas our God like spirit is led by purpose and the Holy Spirit. Our flesh is easily manipulated and wants more control over us than our spirit has. Satan plays on the desires of our flesh to prevent us from tapping into our spirit, which is our direct link to God. Therefore, we not only fast from food, but from anything that distracts us from hearing God's voice clearly. Satan knows that if he can keep our minds in a polluted/distracted state and keep us on the path of pursuing our own desires and not God's purpose for us, then it will be impossible for us to hear God's voice to be led by the spirit. Being led by our selfish desires leads us further away from our purpose and suppresses the voice of the spirit. John 4:24 says *"God is a Spirit, and they that worship him must worship him in spirit"*. Physical praise and worship only, becomes ritual and routine without the spiritual aspect.

John 4:13,
"This is how we know that we live in him and he in us: He has given us his Spirit".

There is a level of alignment that needs to take place to really connect with God on a higher-level. If you are ever feeling distant or disconnected from God, a proper fast is a great place to start aligning your spirit with His for a deeper meaningful connection.

Chapter 6

Carolyn

To fully understand this next section, I'll have to give you a little background information. For a short period of time, I lived in Montgomery Alabama and attended Alabama State University. During that time, God was the furthest thing from my mind. I was not reading my bible or going to church. Truthfully, I was barely going to classes at that point in my life (sorry mom). While in Montgomery, I would frequently perform at a local lounge. This lounge was known more for its spoken word and live instrumentation, but they would sometimes let my friends and I perform our hip hop songs over CD instrumentals. I remember one night, in particular, very clearly. I had just performed two of my songs "Unstoppable" and "Wendy's" and was getting a lot of praise for my performance. As I walked off the stage, a random woman in the crowd handed me a handwritten note and whispered in my ear "God sees you", then proceeded to walk out of the venue. I will never forget this because it was super strange to me. It is important to note that nothing about my performance screamed "God". In fact, my song Wendy's was a song about Netflix and Chilling before Netflix and Chill was a thing. There was a line in my song that said, "...nothings open this late but legs and Wendy's", So after hearing her say, "God sees you" I automatically thought to myself 'Oh, I'm for sure going to hell', but when I opened the note she had handed me, this is what it read:

The Lord says,

Do not aim for the spotlight. There were these mighty men in David's time. Almost nothing is known about them. Except that they were called, 'David's Mighty Men'. To him they were everything. Their blood flows through your veins. You are a Mighty Man. Not just any man, but Gods mighty man. There are Kings and Queens that are destined to flow from your flow. You are not created to be great alone, but to pull others up with you. You are seen. In heaven's stage, you are celebrated and son, that is all you need. God is your audience, and He cheers every time.

P.S. Your heart is amazing!

Love Carolyn

For years I struggled with understanding how she got all of that from my little heathen performance. How did she perceive me as being a mighty man of God from a song like "Wendy's", which was me convincing a girl to come over for the night? What did she see in me that I did not? As time went on, I eventually misplaced the note from Carolyn, but her words stayed with me.

Fast forward 7 years later, I am now living in Dallas, TX, on Day 3 of my fast. It was a very relaxed day, and I was watching a sermon on how God reveals our gifts to us through our passions, while we are still children. It spoke on, how allowing dream killers to speak negative affirmations on our lives can cause us to detour from purpose and abandon our gifts. My phone died mid sermon and since I could not watch TV or any other entertainment due to the fast, the idea popped into my head to reorganize my closet. I decided to start by going through old containers I had been hoarding around since I'd first moved to Texas, and you'll never guess what I found in the very first container I opened. The note I received from Carolyn seven years prior! I read the note from Carolyn again, for the first time in years, and immediately I was hit with complete clarity and under-standing. God's message was so clear to me that I could literally hear Him speaking to me:

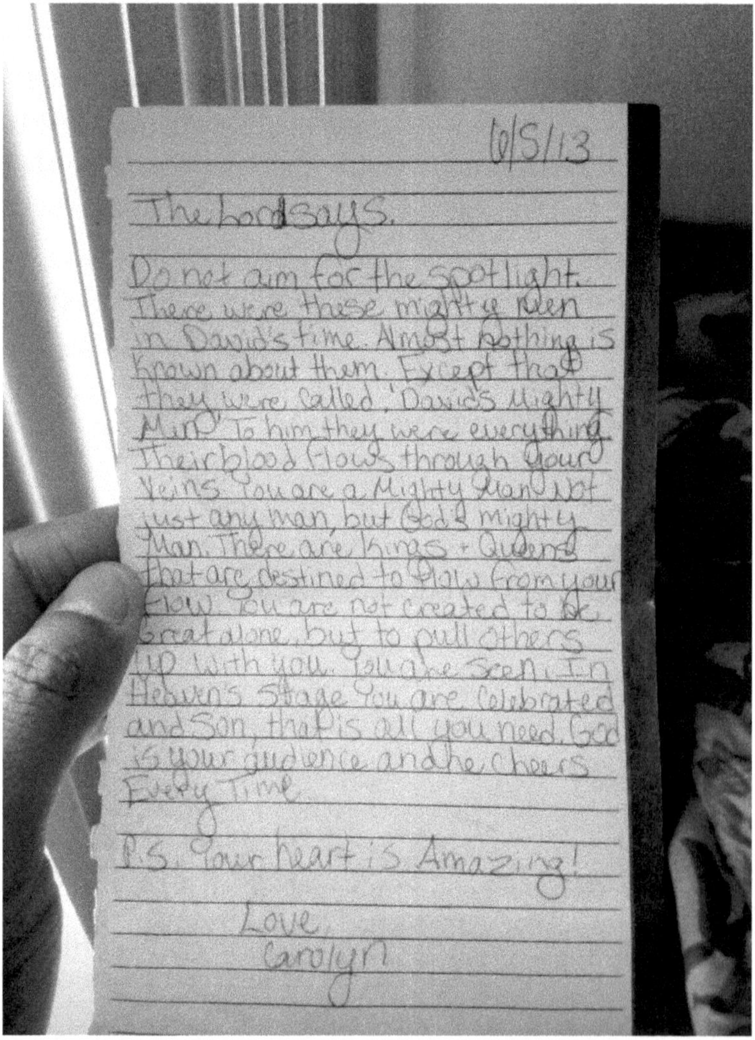

6/5/13

The Lord says,

Do not aim for the spotlight. There were these mighty men in David's time. Almost nothing is known about them. Except that they were called 'David's Mighty Men.' To him they were everything. Their blood flows through your veins. You are a Mighty Man. Not just any man, but God's mighty Man. There are Kings + Queens that are destined to flow from your flow. You are not created to be great alone, but to pull others up with you. You are seen in Heaven's stage. You are celebrated and Son, that is all you need. God is your audience and he cheers Every Time.

P.S. Your heart is Amazing!

Love,
Carolyn

"Do not aim for the spotlight, instead use your music as a tool to get people's attention. What you do with that attention and influence is what you will be judged on. Music is your fruit, and the type of fruit that is produced will determine if your tree is rooted in me or rooted in the world. Music is not your gift. Leadership is your true gift. You will be successful in anything you try, but it is what you do with your influence that will be celebrated in the heavens above. Carolyn was there to plant the seed I knew you were not ready for at the time, but I knew the message would continually pull at your heart knowing that there was a greater calling on your life."

After almost a year hiatus from making music, I decided that day that I would set my home studio back up and create music that pointed people into the direction of The Most High. I did not know how it would translate to my current fans and supporters, but I had peace and confidence knowing that even if no one else accepted it, I would be getting applauded from the heavens above. God's voice was on repeat in my head,

"Music is your fruit, and the type of fruit that is produced will determine if your tree is rooted in me or rooted in the world".

For years I wanted to be the best rapper and impress people with my songs. I got to the point where I was willing to write about anything to get my songs on the radio or placed with a major artist. We often ask for success, but can God trust us to put His plans over our own self-serving plans? We want to be rich and have successful businesses, but why? What are the true intentions in your heart? God only supplies for His purpose and not ours. When it's all said and done, how does your story bring glory and give credit back to Him? I have always been told that I have had leadership qualities, but now that I understand the ability of influence is a gift from God, it was now time to be more intentional about how and where I would lead the people.

Chapter 7

The Voice of God

Up until this point, everything that had been revealed to me had been revealed in the first 4 days of my fast. I was convinced that there was no need to finish off the last 3 days because I had complete clarity on everything I had prayed for. To be honest, I did not think I could go another day without food. I was extremely hungry, and on day 3 I stumbled across a video on what happens to the body during starvation. I had convinced myself that I was dying of starvation (which was the farthest thing from the truth lol). I made the commitment to God that I would seek His presence for 7 days, but I started to justify why it was okay to end my fast on Day 4. I justified this by telling myself that it was not "mission abort" but more like "mission complete" because God had already spoken to me. I was left to make a critical decision, break my fast early or stay committed and trust the process.

On your journey to get closer to God, it is particularly important to be able to recognize God's voice. My question has always been, how do I know that it is God speaking to me and not just my own ideas surfacing? From my experience, the two voices are very similar, but the biggest difference is that our ideas are usually self-serving, and God's commands ultimately bring glory to Him and His purpose for us. God's voice is direct. Yes, He gives us free will, but when He speaks, He does not try to convince you or justify the reasons behind the command. He says what He means, and He means what He says. Here are a few paraphrased examples of how God speaks in scripture:

1. "Abraham take your only son to the mountain top to be sacrificed." (Genesis 22:2)
2. "Saul wait 7 days for Samuel's return before offering the burnt sacrifice" (1 Samuel 10:8)
3. "March around Jericho 7 times." (Joshua 6:4)
4. "Elijah go to Zarephath and find the widow" (1 Kings 17:7-16)
5. The 10 Commandments (Exodus 20)

In the bible we see that whenever God speaks, it is clear and direct, but whenever Satan speaks, it is the exact opposite. When God spoke to Adam, in the garden of Eden, regarding the tree of knowledge, He said, "If you eat its fruit, you are sure to die". Direct and to the point as always! But when the serpent spoke to Eve, he said, "You will not surely die. For God knows that when you eat of it your eyes will be open knowing good and evil". He was speaking to Eve in a convincing manner to justify why she should disobey God's direct order.

To this day, Satan uses the same manipulation and convincing strategies on us that he used on Eve in the beginning. You have to know how to differentiate God's voice and Satan's voice so that you do not mistakenly fulfill Satan's will thinking it is God. God will say, "Do not fornicate", Satan will say "Touching and caressing is ok. If you do not have sex, you surely are not breaking the rules". God will say, "Do not get drunk", Satan will say, "You're only a little tipsy, surely one more glass won't hurt". Be aware of the voice that causes you to drift just enough to fall out of alignment with God. When you start to hear that serpent like voice speaking to you, it is in your best interest to do the opposite.

Chapter 8

Obedience Over Everything

After reflecting on how faithful God had been to me in just 4 days, answering all my prayers, it was a no brainer that I was going to stay committed for the full 7 days of my fast. And that's when the strangest thing happened on Day 5. All those hunger pains I experienced the day before, disappeared, and I was no longer hungry. In fact, I did not have a craving for food that entire day. And to think I was ready to quit and throw in the towel 24 hours prior because I thought I was starving to death. This was a powerful moment for me because it allowed me to see how pointless anxiety and worrying is. Either you trust that God is in full control, or you do not. There is no in-between. The enemy almost caused me to drift, but the spirit was victorious over the flesh. That evening, while I was sitting at my dining room table, drinking hibiscus tea and watching a sermon on YouTube called "Stop Trippin' It's Coming" by Tim Ross, I got the idea to write down everything that had been revealed to me during my fast. This made perfect sense to me because over time we often forget, in detail, what God has revealed/done for us and the storms He has brought us through. This would be my personal journal of His faithfulness, so that I would never forget this journey. I was never big on journals because they reminded me too much of a diary, which seemed super girly, but I decided to get out of my own way and make it happen. I decided, in that moment, that this diary (I mean journal lol) would be something private and for my eyes only. That's when I heard God speak to me in the same way He spoke to me about Carolyn's note. It was clear and direct:

Write a journal detailing your experience during your 7 day fast, sharing the experience and clarity you got from a week of no distractions while seeking my presence. Start by explaining your reasoning behind the fast and what you wanted to get from it. Detail what you were struggling with prior to the fast. Be transparent with the details because there are people going through similar circumstances that will find comfort and strength in hearing your story.

Hear my story? Now I was confused, because I wanted this journal to be for me not the public. I always looked at people sideways who would say that they "Heard from

God" or "God spoke to me". I guess because I had never heard from Him. Prior to this fast, I felt like no one else was really "hearing" from God either. I knew, without a doubt, this was God's voice I was hearing because I would NEVER intentionally share private aspects of my life to the public. I would NEVER randomly have an idea to share intimate aspects of past relationships and the inadequate feeling of not knowing my purpose publicly with other people. The second confirmation which confirmed that it was truly God's voice and not just one of my bright ideas is that I hate writing, especially typing. I would never say "Hey I think it would be cool to write a book". It just would not happen. At this point I was 5 days in without food or distractions, consuming the word of God every chance I got, so it had become a lot easier to hear and accept God's voice. I began to write as instructed.

The Milwaukee hustler in me automatically started thinking about all the different ways I could generate revenue off the book. I started thinking of marketing plans that would get this book to the #1 Best Sellers list. Creative ways to distribute both physical and digital copies. I started thinking about how I could release an audio book on YouTube and generate passive income from monetization. That's when I caught myself. I had started planning the steps of the process without consulting with God and letting Him lay out the plan. If I did not learn anything else during this fast, I learned to pray before everything and let God reveal the vision.

Creating your own vision only leads to years of detours out of alignment with God's purpose for your life. I just sat back in my chair, and I spoke out loud, "God, what is your vision for this book and how should I get it to the people?" I waited a few seconds and here comes that same voice again saying, "Free". I just sat there quietly for another 10 seconds because I know God could not have been talking to me. Free? I may not know what all goes into publishing a book, but I am almost positive that it cost upfront money that is usually recouped on the backend after sales. So, you want me to pour money (that I do not have) into this book and then give it away for free? I just sat there and pretended like I did not hear Him the first time, listening for anything that was more pleasing to my ears. This is what was spoken:

This book will be free. It is not about the money it is about your obedience. This book will be a tool that gets people's attention and brings them closer to me. This book, along with your music, will be the first fruit that comes from your tree that is now rooted in me. Complete the book and more instructions will come after that.

If you are reading this completed book, it is because God provides for His purpose and not for our plans. As I type this, I have no idea how things will pan out, but I know it starts with my obedience.

After 32 years of guessing and making up my own plans, calling it purpose, it only took me 7 days to get the answers I had been looking for. The level of peace I experienced after this fast is a level of peace I cannot explain. When you begin to understand your purpose and allow yourself to be led by the holy spirit, worry and anxiety becomes a thing of the past. If God says go, best believe you have nothing to worry about as long as you go. If God says stop, best believe you have nothing to worry about as long as you stop. The road to peace runs through God. And the road to purpose runs through God. There are no shortcuts or side streets. In a world full of distractions, we must learn to disconnect in order to re-connect. Only then will we find true power, peace, and purpose. I encourage everyone to try fasting while intentionally seeking Gods presence. Worst case scenario, you'll be hungry for a few days and lose a couple pounds. Best case scenario, your life will be changed forever.

Milton Keynes UK
Ingram Content Group UK Ltd.
UKHW020630140823
426838UK00016B/744